Volcanoes
& Earthquakes

SIMON & SCHUSTER BOOKS FOR YOUNG READERS
An imprint of Simon & Schuster Children's Publishing Division
1230 Avenue of the Americas, New York, New York 10020

Conceived and produced by Weldon Owen Pty Ltd
61 Victoria Street, McMahons Point
Sydney, NSW 2060, Australia

Group Chief Executive Officer John Owen
President and Chief Executive Officer Terry Newell
Publisher Sheena Coupe
Creative Director Sue Burk
Concept Development John Bull, The Book Design Company
Editorial Coordinator Mike Crowton
Vice President, International Sales Stuart Laurence
Vice President, Sales and New Business Development Amy Kaneko
Vice President, Sales: Asia and Latin America Dawn Low
Administrator, International Sales Kristine Ravn

Project Editor Lachlan McLaine
Designer Helen Woodward, Flow Design & Communications
Cover Designers Gaye Allen, Kelly Booth, and Brandi Valenza

Color reproduction by Chroma Graphics (Overseas) Pte Ltd
Printed by SNP Leefung Printers Ltd
Manufactured in China

A WELDON OWEN PRODUCTION

The text for this book is set in Meta and Rotis Serif.
10 9 8 7 6 5 4

Library of Congress Cataloging-in-Publication Data
Rubin, Ken, 1962–
Volcanoes & earthquakes / Ken Rubin.
p. cm.
Includes index.

ISBN-13: 978-1-4169-3862-0 (hardcover)
ISBN-10: 1-4169-3862-1 (hardcover)

1. Volcanoes—Juvenile literature. 2. Earthquakes—Juvenile literature. I. Title. II. Title: Volcanoes and earthquakes.
QE521.3.R83 2007
551.21—dc22
2007061745

Volcanoes
& Earthquakes

Ken Rubin

Simon & Schuster Books for Young Readers
New York   London   Toronto   Sydney

Contents

introducing

in focus

introducing

Restless Planet

It might seem to us that nothing is more solid than the ground beneath our feet and that nothing is more permanent than the mountains and the oceans, but in fact our planet is restless and alive. Between Earth's thin rocky crust and its iron core lies the mantle, a zone of very hot, partially molten rock that slowly circulates. This movement pushes and pulls at gigantic slabs of the crust, which are called tectonic plates. This movement can sometimes be felt as earthquakes, and where the plates collide, or where new crust is formed, volcanoes can be found delivering hot molten rock to the surface.

CRUST COMPARED

Earth's crust is composed chiefly of granite and basalt—two types of volcanic rock. Its thickness varies, but it is thinnest on the ocean floor, where it can be only 5 miles (8 km) deep. Over the continents it is up to eight times thicker.

Continental crust

Oceanic crust

History of Earth

Our planet had a hot and fiery birth nearly 4.6 billion years ago. Since then, Earth has cooled and aged and become a cradle for life.

The Earth was born when some of the dust and gas circling the infant Sun came together under the force of gravity.

Shortly after Earth formed it was struck by a small planet. Fortunately the impact was not quite enough to destroy it.

The debris from this huge impact quickly assembled in Earth's orbit to form the Moon.

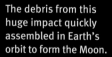

Gradually Earth cooled and an outer crust developed. Volcanoes and comets added water to the atmosphere and oceans formed.

Fire down below

Very soon after Earth formed it separated into layers: a dense, iron-rich core encased within a rocky mantle, surrounded by a hot gaseous atmosphere. With time a crust formed and water condensed to make great oceans. Hot material within the mantle slowly rises toward the crust while cooler material sinks. This motion is called convection.

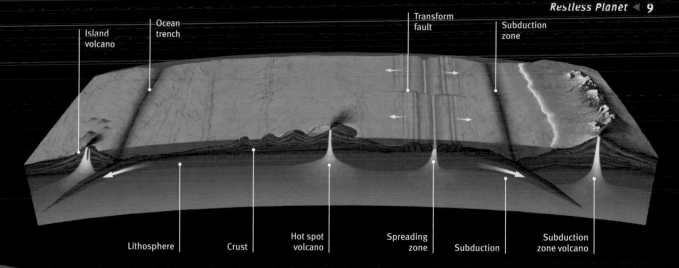

Earth in motion

The oceanic and continental crust (together with the uppermost layer of the upper mantle) form Earth's outer rocky shell, which is called the lithosphere. The lithosphere is divided into many plates that move across the surface of our planet. This movement can sometimes be felt as earthquakes. The movement also forms volcanoes where the lithosphere spreads apart and where plates collide.

Island volcano

Ocean trench

Transform fault

Subduction zone

Lithosphere

Crust

Hot spot volcano

Spreading zone

Subduction

Subduction zone volcano

Crust

Outer mantle

Sinking subduction current

Upper mantle convection current

Lower mantle

Inner core (solid)

Lower mantle convection current

Outer core (molten)

Core convection current

Spreading Seas

Deep beneath the ocean, where one tectonic plate meets another, are giant mountain ranges called mid-ocean ridges. Here, new crust is born and spreads apart. When the crust spreads quickly, the ridge is usually a broad, rounded mountain called a rise, but when the crust moves slowly, most ridges have a deep valley along their tops. No one knew the ocean ridges were there until they were discovered by surveys of the ocean floor in the 1920s. Scientists have now seen them with their own eyes and have discovered an eerie, dark world where superheated water spews from mineral chimneys as high as 15-story buildings and strange forms of life survive.

Fire of the deep

This illustration shows a rift valley at the top of an ocean ridge. Most of the volcanic activity occurs in a narrow (half mile [1 km] or less) zone at the center of the valley. Lava erupts only periodically out of fissures lining the floor while black smoker mineral chimneys can remain active for decades or even centuries.

An ocean is born

The Red Sea (seen here from space) shows where Arabia is pulling away from Africa, splitting open the continental crust. Eventually an ocean may form here, as Africa and Arabia continue to move apart and the volcanic seafloor grows wider.

Terraces *Faulting and lava flooding commonly create steps on rift valley walls.*

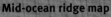

Mid-ocean ridge map

The mid-ocean ridge system (the blue lines on the map above) snakes its way throughout all the ocean basins. The fastest-spreading ridges are in the Pacific, and the slowest are in the Arctic and southwest Indian oceans. On average the plates move apart by about 2.5 inches (6 cm) a year.

NORTH AMERICAN PLATE

EURASIAN PLATE

PACIFIC PLATE

AFRICAN PLATE

INDIAN PLATE

PACIFIC PLATE

NAZCA PLATE

SOUTH AMERICAN PLATE

SOMALI PLATE

AUSTRALIAN PLATE

ANTARCTIC PLATE

Crust spreading

All the continents we recognize today were once joined up in a supercontinent called Pangaea. Over time Pangaea broke apart when upwelling magma split the continental crust and new oceans were born, including the Indian and Atlantic. This process is happening today in parts of eastern Africa.

Faults form when convection currents split the land. The land tilts and drops to create a wide valley between two fault scarps.

When the land drops below sea level, water floods in and fills the valley. Seafloor forms and pushes the landmasses apart.

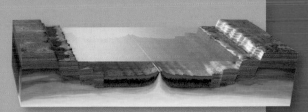

The ocean grows steadily wider as spreading continues. As the seafloor moves outward, it settles and sinks, leaving a high ridge on either side of the rift.

Lava leftovers *Recent eruptions form black pillow lava flows that overlay the older, sediment-covered seafloor.*

Exploring the abyss
Scientists explore mid-ocean ridges using small manned submersibles or with robotic vehicles called ROVs (Remotely Operated Vehicles).

Fiery fissure
Convection currents in Earth's mantle drive the ocean ridge system and bring magma to the surface.

BLACK SMOKER

Hydrothermal chimneys spew out hot, black water containing energy-rich minerals. Colonies of microscopic bacteria feed off these minerals, which in turn support a rich ecosystem of tube worms, blind crabs, and other exotic creatures. Unlike other forms of life on Earth, they do not rely on the energy of the Sun to survive.

Cold seawater seeps into cracks.

Superheated water rises through the chimney.

Tectonic
Collisions

Earth's tallest mountains and deepest ocean trenches form where tectonic plates collide. In many places these collisions form subduction zones—places where old ocean crust is destroyed and returned to the mantle, carrying sediment and seawater with it. The immense forces of colliding plates can melt rock, forming many of Earth's most destructive volcanoes at subduction zones. Continental crust is not dense enough to return to the mantle, so where two continental plates collide, the crust is fractured, folded, and thrust up. Huge mountain ranges, such as the Himalayas and Alps, are formed in this way.

Plate boundaries map
Most collision zones (highlighted in red) ring the vast Pacific Ocean or stretch from Australia to Europe along the margins of an ancient sea called Tethys.

Island arc volcanoes *Where one ocean crust subducts beneath another, the subducting plate begins to melt in the underlying mantle. These are zones of intense volcanic activity and earthquakes.*

Collision of continental plates *The collision of two continental plates folds and crumples the crust into high mountain belts that can change global weather patterns and produce giant landslides.*

CREATION OF THE HIMALAYAS

Earth's highest and youngest mountain range—the Himalayas—was created from a slow but mighty collision between the Indian subcontinent and Asia.

1 **On the move** About 200 million years ago the ancient supercontinent called Pangaea broke up, and India began to move northward.

2 **Big impact** India rammed into Asia about 50 to 40 million years ago, marking the start of Himalayan uplift.

3 **Mountains in motion** Uplift reached full intensity 10 million years ago and continues today.

Mountains and trenches

The forces at work when tectonic plates collide are immense. No other geological process has the power to form the landscape in such dramatic ways.

Mid-plate continental strain *Plate motions can build up enormous stresses within a single plate and cause the land to buckle or fracture.*

Coastal mountains *Continental arc volcanoes sit at the edge of a landmass, above the spot where a subducting ocean plate begins to melt in the mantle.*

Ocean trench *Deep trenches form where an oceanic plate subducts beneath another plate. The deepest places in the ocean are the trenches of the western Pacific.*

Hot Spots

Some of Earth's most magnificent volcanoes and largest outpourings of magma form above hot spots—places where a plume of hot magma pierces the lithosphere like a blowtorch. Most hot spot volcanoes occur away from the edges of Earth's tectonic plates, forming volcanoes that rise up dramatically from the neighboring landscape. A hot spot stays still while the plate above it moves. Over millions of years this produces a line of volcanoes as the plate moves over the hot spot. Hot spot volcanoes are found above both oceanic crust (like Hawaii) and continental crust (like Yellowstone).

Hot spot Hawaii The action of a hot spot and a moving plate is apparent in this photo of the Hawaiian Islands taken from space. Magma is being fed to the large island in the lower right corner. The other islands were formed in the same place but were carried away as the Pacific plate slowly moved to the northwest.

Quiet maturity *Plate motion moves the volcano away from the magma source, and volcanism wanes. Erosion takes over and the island begins to shrink.*

First in line *The volcano closest to the hot spot gets most of the magma supply and grows rapidly.*

Birth of an island *Hot mantle rises and melts at hot spots, creating a ready supply of magma to feed volcanoes above. At oceanic hot spots volcanoes grow from the seafloor to breach the sea surface after about a million years.*

Oceanic hot spot

Volcanoes form, grow, and die as they ride the lithosphere over a mantle hot spot. A single hot spot can send magma to more than one volcano at a time. The combination of a local magma source and a moving plate produces a chain of volcanoes that become progressively older in the direction of plate motion.

Hot spots map

Hot spots occur seemingly randomly all over the globe, beneath both oceans and continents. Although widely distributed, as with volcanoes, their activity levels vary dramatically. Some are dormant but are likely to reawaken in the future.

Fading away *Millions of years later, and hundreds of miles from the hot spot, the once great volcano barely sticks its nose above sea level, but if the ocean is warm enough, a fringing coral reef forms an atoll.*

Returned to the deep *Slowly but surely the plate slides down a subduction zone, taking its remnant hot spot volcanoes back into the mantle.*

Caldera *Infrequent, very large eruptions can drain the magma from beneath the volcano, forming a circular depression called a caldera.*

Ring fault and hills *Hills surrounding a caldera are remnants of the once great volcano that stood there and show where the caldera floor dropped along a ring-shaped fault.*

Continental hot spot

When a hot spot wells up beneath a continental plate, its progress is often slowed down by the weight of crust above it. Huge volumes of magma can accumulate between occasional massive eruptions.

The monster sleeps *A huge magma reservoir—wider than a big city—can form in the crust between eruptions.*

Highest volcanoes by continent

Although many mountains have higher summits, Hawaii's Mauna Kea is the greatest mountain on Earth. Measured from the ocean floor from which it rises, Mauna Kea towers at over 31,000 feet (9,500 m).

Elevation (ft)

Elevation (m)

1. Nevado Ojos del Salado, S. America
   22,664 feet (6,908 m)

2. Kilimanjaro, Africa
   19,331 feet (5,892 m)

3. Damavand, Asia
   18,638 feet (5,681 m)

4. Elbrus, Europe
   18,510 feet (5,642 m)

5. Pico de Orizaba, N. America
   18,406 feet (5,610 m)

6. Mt. Sidley, Antarctica
   13,717 feet (4,181 m)

7. Mauna Kea, Hawaii
   13,717 feet (4,181 m) above sea level
   18,000 feet (5,500 m) below sea level

Anatomy of a
Volcano

When heat deep inside Earth melts rocks, a hot, thick liquid called magma forms. It rises and collects in large underground chambers, where small crystals begin to form, and water and gases separate out as bubbles. Under pressure from the overlying rock, the gases, and fresh magma from below, the magma bursts through cracks in Earth's crust as lava or volcanic ash. Steam, gas, and rock form clouds of smoke during eruptions. Fragments of rock and lava are blown out as volcanic ash and cinder. Small, hot bombs of lava shoot out of the volcano and harden in flight.

Central conduit *The main conduit rises from the magma chamber below. Magma and gases flow up the conduit to erupt through the main vent as lava or volcanic ash.*

Dike *A vertical or near-vertical channel through which magma has pushed its way is called a dike. The magma can break through Earth's surface to form a volcanic vent.*

Fissure eruption *Eruptions that happen from vents aligned along a crack rather than a single opening in the crust are called fissure eruptions. They can reach many miles in length.*

What lies beneath

Within the solid rock of a volcano there are chambers and conduits of molten magma. To determine what is inside a volcano, volcanologists study seismic data, ground deformation, and minerals in the erupted lava.

Crater *Lava, ash, gas, and steam erupt from this funnel-shaped opening at the top or sides of the volcano. Craters range from a few feet to many miles across.*

Side vent *When magma forces its way to the surface along a conduit that does not lead to the main vent, it produces a new opening called a side, or flanking, vent.*

Cone *The cone of the volcano is built up by ash and lava from past eruptions.*

Laccolith *Magma does not always find its way to the surface. Laccoliths are dome-shaped intrusions of magma that can push up overlying layers of rock.*

Types of volcanoes

Volcanoes are classified by the kinds of rock they are made of, by their shape, and by their eruption history. Conditions at Earth's surface during eruptions, whether they involve air, water, or ice, also affect the type of volcano that is formed.

Cinder cone Mildly explosive eruptions build up cone-shaped hills of volcanic cinders around a central vent. Eruptions that form cinder cones sometimes end with lava flows that can fill the crater.

Composite or stratovolcano These tall, steep-sided volcanoes are formed when multiple eruptions deposit alternating layers of volcanic ash and lava. They are widely admired for their conical shape.

Shield Volcanoes formed entirely from lava that flows radially from a central vent are called shield volcanoes. These broad volcanoes can form from single eruptions or from many thousands of them.

Fissure and rift A linear fracture of Earth's surface through which magma has erupted forms a fissure volcano. Alternating eruptions and spreading of the rock on either side of the fissure forms a rift volcano.

VEI: 0 1 2 3 4 5 6 7 8 9

1. Kilauea, Hawaii 1983–present
2. Stromboli, Italy c.2000 BC–present
3. Nevado del Ruiz, Colombia 1985
4. Mt. St. Helens, USA 1980
5. Vesuvius, Italy AD 79
6. Pinatubo, Philippines 1991
7. Krakatau, Indonesia 1881
8. Tambora, Indonesia 1815
9. Taupo, New Zealand AD 186
10. Toba, Indonesia 73,000 years ago

Volcanic Explosivity Index

The Volcanic Explosivity Index (VEI) is a scale used to categorize the size and power of eruptions. The VEI uses a logarithmic scale, meaning that an increase of one on the scale represents a tenfold increase in eruption size and power. The location and VEIs of some famous eruptions are shown on the left.

Types of Eruptions

Volcanoes erupt in many ways, emitting a combination of gases, lava, and fragmented rock particles called pyroclasts. Eruptions can shoot out from a central vent or multiple vents, which are called fissures if the vents lie along a line. The type of eruption depends on many factors, such as how much magma has accumulated within the volcano, magma temperature and composition, and whether or not water is present (such as in a lake or an ocean). Volcanologists recognize two main types of eruptions: effusive, when lava flows gently from the volcano; and explosive, when huge clouds of material violently shoot out from the volcano and subsequently fall to the ground.

Plinian

Named after the ancient Roman Pliny the Younger, who described the Mount Vesuvius eruption in AD 79, Plinian eruptions can shoot material 30 miles (45 km) high and disperse material far and wide. A special class called Ultraplinian occurs very rarely but is even more powerful.

MEASURING ERUPTIVE VOLUME

The amount of material ejected by a volcano gives a good indication of its overall power. Eruptive volumes can vary widely, from small house-size deposits to something tens of millions times larger.

670 mi³ (2800 km³)
Toba
VEI: 9

24 mi³ (100 km³)
Taupo
VEI: 8

19 mi³ (80 km³)
Tambora
VEI: 7

4.25 mi³ (18 km³)
Krakatau
VEI: 6

2.4 mi³ (10 km³)
Pinatubo
VEI: 6

0.7 mi³ (3 km³)
Vesuvius
VEI: 5

0.25 mi³ (1 km³)
Mt. St. Helens
VEI: 5

Hawaiian
Named for the Hawaiian Islands, these eruptions mainly produce lava flows—and occasionally lava lakes—from hot, runny magma. The gas-rich early stages can produce fire fountains that reach 3,000 feet (1 km) high.

Strombolian
Named for the Italian volcano Stromboli, these eruptions produce explosions of glowing rock that can reach 600 feet (200 m) into the air before falling to the ground close to the vent.

Up in smoke
Many types of eruptions are named after the characteristics of a famous volcano. But each eruption is a little different, and any volcano can experience different eruption types during its active lifetime.

Vulcanian
Named for the Italian volcano Vulcano, these eruptions are small in volume but can shoot ash and cinders up to an altitude of 15 miles (20 km), dispersing material over a greater area than Strombolian eruptions.

Peleean
Named for Mount Pelée on the island of Martinique, these eruptions are like Vulcanian or Plinian ones but also produce large, fast-moving, gravity-driven flows of hot gas, rock, and ash when domes of thick lava suddenly collapse.

Surtseyan
These eruptions are named after Surtsey, an island formed in 1963 off the coast of Iceland. In Surtseyan eruptions, large quantities of shallow seawater interact with hot magma to build a cone of rock fragments. If the eruption continues long enough, the vent becomes protected from seawater and the eruptions become less violent.

Lava and Ash

No two volcanoes or eruptions are exactly alike, but what they all do is spew very hot material from one or more vents that connect their hot interiors with the surface. This material can include molten lava, gas, ash, and solidified rocks called blocks and bombs. Some volcanic eruptions build up thick piles of lava or pyroclastic rock close to their vent, but others send their materials far and wide, especially when the eruption column rises high into the atmosphere. Even when they are not erupting, volcanoes can emit large quantities of gas from smaller vents known as fumaroles and superheated water from gurgling volcanic springs.

Ash distribution
Volcanic ash sometimes rises in tall plumes into the stratosphere. Here it can be swept great distances by the prevailing winds.

Lava tube breakout *Lava can flow for many miles through lava tubes before emerging at the surface.*

Fire curtain *Fluid lava can erupt through a line of vents (a fissure) to make a curtain of fire.*

Aa flow *This type of lava flow (pronounced "ah-ah") was named by the Hawaiians for its rough, jumbled, jagged surface.*

Lava danger *Almost all lava moves slowly enough that people can escape the danger. However, trees, buildings, signs, and cars will ignite when overrun by the red-hot liquid.*

FORMATION OF A LAVA TUBE

Sometimes lava travels through sub-surface channels that can become tubular caves when the flow is exhausted.

1 A river of molten lava flows in an open channel down the side of a volcano.

Hot lava flow

2 With time the upper surface and sides of the channel begin to cool and coalesce, forcing the flow through the center of the channel.

Lava river

3 Eventually the entire upper surface cools to a solid crust, leaving a subterranean lava flow that can travel great distances in this insulated tube.

Hard tube

4 When the eruption stops and the lava drains away, a hollow tunnel called a lava tube is left behind. These can be higher and wider than train tunnels.

Lava bomb *Chunks of once molten rock can cool and solidify as they fly through the air to become solid lava bombs that can take many distinctive aerodynamic shapes.*

Fireworks *Often very hot and fluid lava is charged with gas when it first breaks the surface early in an eruption, and it comes shooting out like an exploding can of soda. Red-hot lava can spurt up to 600 feet (200 m) in the air from a circular vent to produce a fire fountain.*

Eruption in progress

An erupting volcano is a dramatic and sometimes beautiful spectacle to watch from a safe distance, but it can also be dangerous and very destructive. This illustration shows many different types of eruptions and a variety of volcanic deposits, but we would never see a real volcano doing all of these things at once.

Pyroclastic flow *These superheated currents of hot gas and ash shoot rapidly down the side of a volcano during an eruption.*

Ash fall

After lying dormant for centuries the sleeping Soufrière Hills volcano on the Caribbean island of Montserrat came alive with a series of ash eruptions in 1995. The island's capital of Plymouth was abandoned in 1997 after it was buried by ash and pyroclastic flows.

Pahoehoe flow *The ancient Hawaiians gave us this word for lava that flows smoothly over the ground surface to produce a flat, or sometimes gently folded, surface that can look like coils of rope.*

Volcanic
Landscapes

Volcanoes have helped shape Earth's crust since the planet was born, producing dramatic mountains, craters, and plateaus, as well as rolling hills, islands, and fertile farmlands. It is easy to identify a volcano when it is erupting, or by its distinctive shape or deposits if it is dormant or recently extinct. But volcanism can leave its mark on the landscape even hundreds of millions of years after the eruptions have ceased. Often the clues are quite subtle and it takes the trained eye of a geologist to spot them.

Dormant volcano *Some volcanoes can lie quiet for many centuries between eruptions, allowing plants, animals, and people to live on the rich land in the mountain's shadow. Yet volcanoes that awaken infrequently are some of the most dangerous.*

Volcanic island *Volcanoes that form beneath the sea can grow to create islands. If a volcano stops growing before it reaches the surface, it is called a seamount.*

Living with volcanoes *Volcanic soil is usually very rich and, in spite of the danger, the areas near volcanoes are often densely populated.*

Land made from fire

This is an imaginary landscape, but the volcanic features shown can be found all over the world. You can be thousands of miles away from the closest active volcano and still be surrounded by volcanic landforms.

Caldera formation

Calderas often form as an intermediate stage between repeated eruptions and can often be recognized millions of years after the volcano is extinct.

Major eruptions can release huge volumes of magma from the chamber beneath a volcano.

Continued eruption can partially empty the chamber, leaving an empty space beneath the volcano.

A large caldera is formed when the weight of the volcano collapses along ring faults and falls into the chamber.

Caldera *Magma and gas can accumulate in large chambers beneath a volcano. When the magma drains out or is erupted, a giant cavity remains that often collapses to form a crater called a caldera.*

Volcanic dike *Some of the world's most dramatic geological structures are monuments to long-dead volcanoes whose softer outer layers have eroded away, revealing harder rock from the interior.*

Crater lake *Some calderas fill with water to become lakes that may be tens of miles across. Volcanic gases and geothermal waters often give these lakes unusual colors and chemistries.*

Great flood *Very occasionally, immense quantities of lava pour out of long fissures in Earth's surface and produce vast lava plains that flood the landscape. After hundreds of these eruptions, a plateau many miles thick is formed. Later, erosion and faulting form steep terraced hills.*

Spire and dike formation

Spires and dikes can be amazing natural structures. They come about through a combination of volcanism and erosion.

Hot magma fills the internal columns and pipes of an active volcano.

When the volcano has finished its active life, any magma remaining cools and forms hard rock.

Millions of years later, erosion of the softer surrounding rocks will reveal these structures.

Thermal Springs and
Geysers

Almost everywhere on Earth, temperatures increase the deeper it is below the surface. This is especially so near volcanoes. When groundwater circulates through hot rock, it heats up, becomes less dense, and then tries to force its way to the surface. Places where hydrothermal waters naturally vent on the surface are called thermal springs. Occasionally, subterranean chambers become filled and pressurized with hot water that periodically bursts forth on the surface in an explosion of water called a geyser. In some countries scientists and engineers use this hot water to heat homes and to make electricity. It is one of the cleanest ways of generating power because the main byproduct is steam.

Simian spring
It is not only people who enjoy bathing in thermal springs. This troop of Japanese macaques are famous for escaping the winter cold in the thermal springs near the Shiga Kogen volcano in Japan.

Steam world
Hydrothermal areas can be found on land and beneath the sea, with water temperatures ranging from hot tap water to boiling water or even hotter steam. The waters can be rich with unusual chemical salts and often carry the rotten-egg smell of hydrogen sulfide gas.

Rock power *Geothermal power stations use hot thermal waters brought up from below to generate electricity or hot water for nearby towns.*

Waterworks *Cold water is injected down a well into a geothermal reservoir, where it is heated and returned to the power plant. Geothermal water is usually too salty to use directly in electricity generation, so huge coils of pipes are used to transfer the heat to freshwater to drive the turbines.*

Hot mud *Long-term continuous discharge of geothermal water can turn the surrounding rock into thick mud, forming gurgling "mud pots" or "mud cauldrons" at the thermal spring.*

Stages of a geyser
Geysers are a very rare phenomenon because at least three specific conditions must exist: plenty of groundwater; geothermal heat; and pressure- and watertight plumbing.

Groundwater heats up when it approaches hot rock and magma.

Cold water from above acts like a lid on the hot water below and pressure begins to build.

Eventually the pressure of the hot water exceeds that of the cold water and the system bursts forth as a boiling geyser.

Sculpted by water *Many geothermal areas feature terraces of carbonate, silicate, or sulfide minerals deposited from the hot waters.*

What a rush *Geysers are periodic explosions of geothermal water from beneath the surface. Old Faithful in Yellowstone National Park (USA) and Geysir (southwestern Iceland) are two famous examples.*

Spring into it *Many thermal springs are popular vacation spots, especially where hot water mixes with cooler river or lake water to produce water of more comfortable temperature for bathing.*

Where the geyser sleeps
Below every geyser is a subterranean cavity that fills up with water and gases between each geyser eruption.

Volcanologists
In the Field

Volcanologists are scientists who study volcanoes using methods from geology, chemistry, geography, mineralogy, physics, and sociology to understand how volcanoes form, when and how often they might erupt, and how eruptions affect people and the landscape. An important part of a volcanologist's work happens in the field, where many different measurements are made to learn about what a volcano is doing or did in the past. Other measurements are made in the laboratory or by the watchful eyes of satellites. It takes dedicated teams of scientists to gather and interpret all of this data, which is used to keep people informed about volcanic hazards.

Volcanologists at work

Volcanologists bring many special tools to the field for volcano study. Active volcanoes are dynamic and exciting workplaces, but volcanologists must prepare carefully for field work and always be aware of the hazards.

Survey says *Careful surveys are made to detect the slightest changes in a volcano's topography. A bulge in the surface may indicate that an eruption is on the way.*

The easy way up *Helicopters help volcanologists reach remote volcanoes and cover lots of ground, but pilots need special skills to navigate the often rugged terrain and hot, particle-filled air.*

It's a gas *The complex mix of gases that vent from a volcano are sucked into a vacuum chamber, sealed, and returned to the lab for chemical analysis.*

Electronic nose *Scientists use a correlation spectrometer to measure sulfur dioxide emitted from a volcano. Monitoring this dangerous gas helps scientists understand what is happening inside the volcano.*

Clues in the rock

Volcanologists often take rock samples to the laboratory to study their internal structure, mineralogy, and composition. One way to do this is to view a thin slice of rock under a polarizing light microscope, which reveals minerals in vivid color.

Watch out! *Volcanologists never know when a small explosion might send hot rock fragments or gases their way, so they work in teams and keep a close watch on their surroundings.*

Hot work *You really feel the heat when you are up close and personal with a 2,200°F (1,200°C) lava flow. Specially designed thermal suits keep volcanologists cool when they sample molten lava.*

When the
Earth Moves

If you feel a shaking, bouncing, or rocking motion of the ground, you are probably experiencing an earthquake. Earthquakes, and milder tremors, occur whenever rocks on either side of deep faults in Earth's crust suddenly break and slide past each other. The strength and duration of earthquakes depend on many factors, such as how deep in Earth the rupture was, how much stress the rocks were feeling before the fault slipped, and the kinds of rocks involved. Many earthquakes occur because some rocks in the crust resist the movements deep within Earth that cause plates to separate, collide, and slide past each other. Other quakes occur when huge weights build upon or are rapidly removed from the crust.

The Richter scale
American seismologist Charles Richter developed this earthquake magnitude scale in 1935. Each step on the scale represents a tenfold increase in earthquake power. That means that magnitude 7 is 10 times stronger than magnitude 6, and 100 times stronger than magnitude 5.

Broken earth
About 500,000 earthquakes are detected in the world each year. Most are too mild to be felt by people, but about 100 a year are strong enough to cause damage.

KINDS OF FAULTS

Faults are cracks in the crust where rock has moved at least once in the past. They are classified by the direction of their motion. Movement along faults is often a slow creep, but larger, sudden shifts produce earthquakes. The biggest quakes rupture the surface and deform the ground.

Epicenter This is the point on the surface directly above the hypocenter.

Normal fault Rocks on one side of the fault slump lower than on the other side.

Thrust or reverse fault The rocks on one side of the fault are thrust up above those on the other side.

Hypocenter The hypocenter is where energy in strained rocks is suddenly released as earthquake waves.

Transcurrent or strike-slip fault Rocks on either side of the fault slide past each other.

The modified Mercalli scale
Introduced in 1902 by Italian volcanologist Giuseppe Mercalli, the Mercalli scale measures earthquake intensity by the local effects on Earth's surface. As with the Richter scale, the modified Mercalli scale (so called because of its many updates) is often used to describe earthquakes to the public, but seismologists have now developed new measures of seismic energy.

I	II	III	IV	V
Instrumental	**Feeble**	**Slight**	**Moderate**	**Rather strong**
Felt by very few people; barely noticeable	Felt by a few people, especially on upper floors	Noticeable indoors, especially on upper floors; hanging objects swing	Felt by many indoors, few outdoors; dishes, windows, and doors rattle	Felt by almost everyone, sleeping people wake; small objects moved; trees and poles may shake

VI
Strong
elt by everyone; difficult to walk; some heavy furniture moved; some plaster falls; chimneys may be slightly maged

VII
Very Strong
Difficult to stand; slight to moderate damage in well-built, ordinary structures; considerable damage to poorly built structures; some chimneys broken

VIII
Destructive
Considerable damage to ordinary buildings; severe damage to poorly built structures; heavy furniture overturned; some walls collapse

IX
Ruinous
Considerable damage to specially built structures; buildings shifted off foundations; ground cracked noticeably; underground pipes crack

X
Disastrous
Most masonry and frame structures and their foundations destroyed; ground badly cracked; landslides; railroad tracks bend

XI
Very Disastrous
Few, if any, structures standing; bridges destroyed; wide cracks in ground; waves seen on ground

XII
Catastrophic
Total destruction; ground moves in waves; heavy objects thrown in the air

Earthquake
Preparation

Strong and gentle, extended and brief, tremors and quakes shake our Earth many times each day. We know how and why earthquakes and tremors occur, but not how to predict or prevent this awesome force of nature. But we can prepare for the inevitable. Studies of past earthquake frequency, type, size, ground rupture patterns, and building damage allow seismologists and engineers to select less-hazardous sites for buildings and roads, and to design structures better able to withstand the swaying, rolling, or pogo-stick motions of earthquakes. Being prepared also means having an efficient plan for responding to earthquake-related emergencies immediately after they happen.

AMAZING PAGODAS

Many of Japan's Buddhist pagodas have stood for more than a thousand years, surviving countless earthquakes that have destroyed buildings around them. Modern engineers have only recently unraveled the ancient secrets of their design.

Jiggling joints
The flexible timber parts of a pagoda are slotted together without nails. During an earthquake they jostle about, dissipating the seismic energy.

Swingers The five stories of a pagoda can swing independently of one another. During an earthquake the pagoda does a kind of "snake dance," keeping the building balanced.

Hard knocks
A massive central pillar dampens the vibration when the stories move.

Top-heavy *A tuned mass damper is a heavy weight installed at the top of a tall building. It is designed to move in the opposite direction of the building, keeping it steady when the wind blows or the ground shakes.*

Braced for the worst
Diagonal cross-bracing stops the building from moving more than it should.

Training for tremors
In some parts of the world, earthquake drills are a regular part of school life. Underneath a desk is a safe place to get to when an earthquake starts.

Shaken, not disturbed

Every year architects and engineers discover ways to build earthquake-resistant structures and to improve the safety of older ones. But these technologies are expensive, and tragically, earthquakes in less-developed regions of the world still regularly cause massive loss of life and property.

All together now In many earthquake-prone cities engineers have put electricity, gas, water, and telephone lines together in a single, specially strengthened tunnel.

Pillar of strength Concrete columns reinforced with spirals of steel are good at resisting the flexing and shaking forces of an earthquake.

Slip and slide A linear slider foundation allows the whole building to move horizontally, dissipating energy rather than breaking apart.

Bouncy building This connection between the building and its foundation allows the building to bounce up and down during an earthquake.

After an Earthquake

Earthquakes can cause terrible death and destruction, particularly if the quake is large or affects a densely populated area. Big quakes destroy buildings, rupture pipelines, and shut down electric power plants, all of which greatly disrupts urban life. Earthquake waves pass quickly through hard bedrock, but soft sediments and soils can momentarily turn into a liquid-like state. Because of this, earthquake damage can vary widely over small distances in a city. After the quake, fires and the lack of fresh water and functioning sewer systems can turn things from bad to worse.

Fire damage *Fires fueled by broken gas lines, ruptured fuel tanks, and chemical spills often follow an earthquake and can cause more death and destruction than the quake itself.*

Salvation from above *When roads and railways are broken or obstructed, helicopters may be the only way of getting in and out of an earthquake disaster zone.*

Eye spy *Rescuers use a small "snake eye" camera with a flexible cable to search for victims buried beneath the rubble.*

Breath of life *Trapped people can be located by detecting faint carbon dioxide signals from their exhaled breath.*

Liquefaction *Intense, rapid shaking can turn soft sediments and soil into a liquid-like slurry, causing buildings and other structures built above to sink or collapse.*

People first

Rescuing the living and tending to the wounded are the first things on the minds of rescue teams after a natural disaster such as an earthquake. People trapped inside buildings may have limited air supply or access to water, so rescue work proceeds with a sense of urgency.

Earthmovers *Landslides are another earthquake hazard. Entire towns have been buried beneath loosened soil and rocks.*

Big crunch *Poorly built multistory buildings can sometimes collapse like a house of cards.*

Water to waste *Clean water is essential for survival, and firefighters need a good supply to do their job. Broken water mains can be a big problem after a quake.*

SEARCH-AND-RESCUE DOGS

Search-and-rescue dogs use their powerful sense of smell to help locate victims in the rubble after an earthquake. Many different breeds are used, but all dogs must undergo extensive training for this important job. When disaster strikes, search-and-rescue dogs and their handlers come from all over the world to help.

Ear to the ground *The slightest noise made by a victim can be picked up with extra-sensitive microphones. By using more than one microphone, rescuers can identify a victim's exact location.*

The Making of a
Tsunami

Tsunamis—the name is Japanese for "great harbor waves"— are caused by a jolt to the ocean floor from an earthquake, volcanic eruption, or landslide. These giant waves may travel for thousands of miles but remain unnoticed as they pass under ships. A rise in the ocean floor near a coastline acts as a brake at the bottom of the wave. This forces the tsunami to slow down and rush upward, sometimes as towering walls of water called "wave trains" that crash onto land. The power of the waves batters and floods the coast, and can cause enormous damage and loss of life.

Submarine earthquake

Most tsunamis form when an earthquake occurs deep in the ocean. Tectonic plates grind together, Earth's crust moves, water is disturbed, and powerful shock waves form.

Tsunami disasters

1. 1946 Alaskan quake generates a tsunami. Hours later it kills 159 people in Hawaii.
2. 1964 Waves from an Alaskan quake kill 122 as they sweep down the West Coast.
3. 1896 A tsunami hits Los Angeles on the Californian coast.
4. 1960 A tsunami kills 1,000 in Chile and 61 in Hawaii.
5. 1775 An earthquake in Lisbon generates a tsunami. More than 60,000 die.
6. 1883 Krakatau erupts and a tsunami sweeps over Indonesia. 36,000 people die.
7. 2004 A powerful earthquake triggers waves that travel thousands of miles to crash onto the coastlines of at least 14 Asian and African countries. More than 225,000 people die.
8. 1976 A tsunami kills more than 5,000 people in the Philippines.
9. 1998 A tsunami strikes the north coast of Papua New Guinea, killing 2,000 people.
10. 1896 The Sanriku tsunami strikes Japan and kills more than 26,000 people.

Spiraling forces *The powerful shock waves of energy spread out, rather like ripples when a stone is thrown into a pond. The waves can race across oceans for thousands of miles at speeds of up to 500 miles (800 km) an hour—as fast as a jet plane.*

Before the tsunami
There is no sign of danger, but a tsunami can travel across an entire ocean in just one day. Early-warning systems are making it easier for scientists to predict when and where a tsunami will hit.

Water retreats
The peaceful bay is drained, as if someone had pulled a giant bath plug and let the water out. Bay water meets the developing tsunami just offshore.

Disaster strikes
The water rushes back to the beach. Walls of water, up to 100 feet (30 m) high, crash on the shore and push inland with unstoppable force.

Unknown terror *On the surface all seems calm. The tsunami may be less than 40 inches (1 m) high and is hardly noticed by sailors at sea as it moves beneath the surface.*

At the shore *As the waves move closer to the shore, their speed decreases and their height increases. The tsunami arrives as a series of crests and troughs, between 10 and 45 minutes apart.*

Seismologists
In the Field

Seismologists are scientists who study earthquakes. They use information from geology, physics, civil engineering, and geography to understand the reasons why earthquakes occur and the damage they cause. Seismologists also work with engineers to improve building codes and construction methods to make cities safer. Fieldwork is an important part of seismology. Many different measurements are made to learn about ground motion and deformation around earthquake faults, past and present. Other measurements are made in the laboratory to determine how materials behave when they encounter seismic waves.

Seismic waves
Energy generated by an earthquake travels in the form of waves through the surrounding rock. There are four kinds of seismic waves: two waves that travel through the interior of Earth, and two slower, more destructive waves that travel just under Earth's surface.

P-waves Primary, or pressure, waves pulse quickly through Earth's interior to the surface. These are the first waves felt in an earthquake.

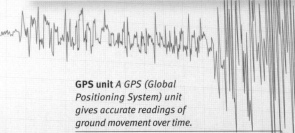

GPS unit *A GPS (Global Positioning System) unit gives accurate readings of ground movement over time.*

ANIMAL INSTINCT

Many people, since at least the time of the ancient Greeks, have observed strange animal behavior in the hours before an earthquake and have concluded that the animals could sense what was to come. It is unclear what they might be sensing and how. One theory is that animals can detect small changes in Earth's local magnetic field that are known to precede a quake. Unfortunately, scientific tests of earthquake occurrences and patterns of animal behavior have not yet found a particular animal response that is reliable enough to predict earthquakes.

Magnetometer *A magnetometer detects the direction or intensity of Earth's magnetic field. Earthquakes are often preceded by small, ultralow-frequency variations in the local magnetic field.*

Seismometer *This instrument detects the direction and intensity of seismic waves produced by earthquakes. The location and magnitude of a quake can be determined from the records of multiple seismometers.*

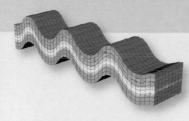

S-waves Secondary, or shear, waves shift material sideways as they propagate through Earth's interior at about half the speed of P-waves.

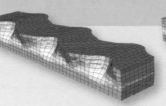

Love waves Love waves are side-to-side shearing motions of Earth's surface. They move more slowly than P- or S-waves.

Rayleigh waves Rayleigh waves cause the ground surface to deform like waves on the ocean. These are the slowest of the four seismic wave types.

Satellite laser ranging *Seismologists aim laser beams at mirrors mounted on satellites to detect small movements before or after a quake.*

Seismic truck *These trucks create seismic waves by thumping the ground with a hydraulic piston. Equipment in a monitoring van records how the waves travel through the ground.*

Ancient seismometer
The ancient Chinese scientist and inventor Zhang Heng produced a device for detecting tremors in the year AD 132. When disturbed, a pendulum within the bronze chamber caused a dragon's mouth to open and drop a ball into the mouth of a toad.

With a trace *Traditionally seismometers recorded earthquakes and tremors by drawing a line on a moving strip of paper. Today, nearly all seismometers record directly to computer memory.*

Borehole strain meter *These devices are placed in deep holes in the rock around earthquake faults. They measure the amount of stress on the rocks and how the rocks are deforming.*

Creepmeter *A creepmeter measures the slow movement or deformation of rock under stress below the surface.*

Seismologists at work

The seismologists' tool kit is full of specialized gear to study earthquake faults and ground motion. But they also need simple tools, such as a hammer to break up rocks, and a shovel to dig trenches into surface faults.

Locator map This map of the world shows you exactly where the featured event occurred. Look for the large red dot on each map.

THE SAN FRANCISCO EARTHQUAKE

DATE: **April 18, 1906**

DURATION: **45–60 seconds**

RICHTER SCALE: **7.8–8.3**

MERCALLI SCALE: **VII–IX**

DEATH TOLL: **478 (official); 3,000–6,000 (estimated)**

Fast facts Fast facts at your fingertips give you essential information on each event being explored.

VEI 9

VEI 8

VEI 7

VEI 6

VEI 5

VEI 4

VEI 3

VEI 2

VEI 1

Side bar This side bar indicates how powerful the event was as measured by Volcanic Explosivity Index (volcanoes) or Richter scale (earthquakes).

VEI 9

VEI 8

VEI 7

VEI 6

VEI 5

VEI 4

VEI 3

VEI 2

VEI 1

TOBA: THE FACTS

DATE: Approximately 73,500 years ago

VOLCANIC EXPLOSIVITY INDEX: 9

ERUPTION TYPE: Ultra-Plinian

ERUPTIVE VOLUME: Approximately 670 cubic miles (2,800 km³)

DEATH TOLL: Unknown

Awesome ash cloud Ash spread far and wide during the Toba eruption, leaving deposits 30 feet (9 m) thick in Malaysia and up to 6 inches (15 cm) thick in far-off India and the Bay of Bengal.

Toba

Visit peaceful Lake Toba on the Indonesian island of Sumatra today, and you would never realize you were standing at the site of the largest volcanic eruption in human history. The lake is actually a caldera about 55 miles long by 20 miles across (90 x 30 km). Scientists believe that around 73,500 years ago it unleashed a catastrophic eruption that spread volcanic ash and gases across the globe. The eruption probably lasted only a couple of weeks, but its effects were widely felt as a dramatic global cooling that lasted six years. This brought about changes to landscapes, forests, and wildlife during a critical period of human development.

Longest winter

After the Toba eruption, our Stone Age ancestors must have suffered greatly from long, cold years of reduced food supply. Some scientists have speculated that this eruption brought humans to the brink of extinction.

Toba today The Lake Toba region is still volcanically active. Samosir Island, in the middle of the lake, is being pushed up out of the water by a swelling dome of magma beneath it. It is now the largest island within an island on Earth.

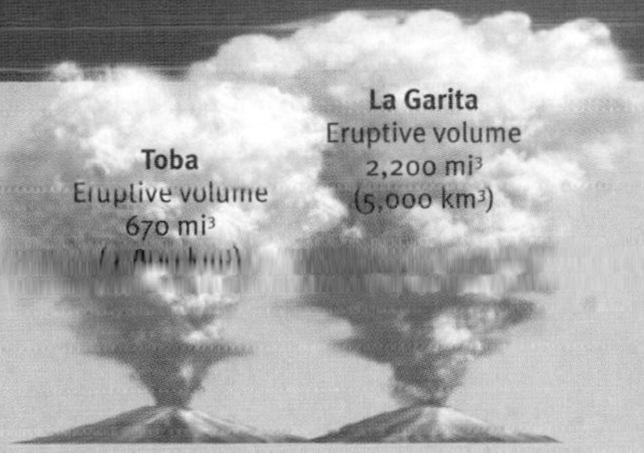

Toba
Eruptive volume
670 mi³
(2,800 km³)

La Garita
Eruptive volume
2,200 mi³
(5,000 km³)

Biggest bang The Toba eruption was the biggest that humans have ever lived through, but it is not the largest volcanic eruption we know of. The La Garita eruption in the western United States some 27 million years ago was almost twice as big.

Deadly haze Volcanic ash and sulfur dioxide aerosols injected into the stratosphere formed a thin layer surrounding the globe, partially blocking the Sun's warming rays. This caused a long volcanic winter.

Altitude

mi	km
15	25
	20
10	15
	10
5	5
0	0

VEI 9

VEI 8

VEI 7

VEI 6

VEI 5

VEI 4

VEI 3

VEI 2

VEI 1

VESUVIUS: THE FACTS

DATE: AD 79

VOLCANIC EXPLOSIVITY INDEX: 5

ERUPTION TYPE: Plinian/Vulcanian

ERUPTIVE VOLUME: Approximately 0.7 cubic miles (3.3 km³)

DEATH TOLL: Between about 3,000 and 10,000

Escape from Herculaneum

In the 1980s, archaeologists uncovered about 250 human skeletons huddled together inside boathouses on the ancient shore. This discovery enabled them to re-create exactly what was happening when Herculaneum was destroyed.

Putting to sea *Boats were probably the best means of escape—even in the tempestuous seas. Presumably the people in the boathouses were awaiting their turn to leave.*

Vesuvius

Nearly two thousand years ago, Mount Vesuvius in Italy erupted and destroyed the towns of Pompeii and Herculaneum. The eruption started with a huge column of ash rising high into the sky. It was followed the next day by a pyroclastic flow that famously buried two cities and killed many of their residents who were unable to flee. Hidden for centuries beneath the ash, the cities were rediscovered and excavated beginning in the 1600s, providing the world with an archaeological treasure and a detailed record of how people lived in ancient Roman times.

CASTS OF HUNDREDS

Pompeii and Herculaneum became time capsules beneath the ash, preserving every detail of the towns when Vesuvius erupted. In Pompeii, these details include casts of the people who died that day.

1 Thousands of people in Pompeii were suffocated by volcanic ash and gases. As the ash piled up, their bodies were entombed.

2 Soon the bodies decayed, leaving behind skeletons, jewelry, and other hard objects in the body-shaped cavities. Centuries later when archaeologists discovered the cavities, they carefully filled them with plaster.

3 When the ash was removed, perfect casts of the victims were revealed. Many have been left in place, while others are in museums.

Menacing water *Violent winds from the eruption column and rumbling earthquakes below created turbulent and stormy seas in the Bay of Naples.*

Ash fall *Suffocating hot ash and pumice fell from the spreading eruption cloud. Herculaneum was eventually buried under about 60 feet (18 m) of volcanic deposits that hardened like concrete.*

No escape *Almost all human remains found in Herculaneum have been uncovered in the town's boathouses. The people were killed instantly when the pyroclastic flow swept in from Vesuvius.*

Witness to disaster

One witness to the eruption was the seventeen-year-old Gaius Plinius Caecilius Secundus (Pliny the Younger), who was on the opposite side of the Bay of Naples. His account is the earliest eyewitness record of a volcanic eruption.

August 24: afternoon

"The cloud was rising from a mountain.... I can best describe its shape by likening it to a pine tree. It rose into the sky on a very long 'trunk' from which spread some 'branches.'"

August 24: evening

"Ash was falling onto the ships now, darker and denser the closer they went. Now it was bits of pumice, and rocks that were blackened and burned and shattered by the fire."

August 25: morning

"It wasn't long thereafter that the cloud stretched down to the ground and covered the sea. It girdled Capri and made it vanish, it hid Misenum's promontory."

VEI 9
VEI 8
VEI 7
VEI 6
VEI 5
VEI 4
VEI 3
VEI 2
VEI 1

KRAKATAU: THE FACTS

DATE: August 27, 1883

VOLCANIC EXPLOSIVITY INDEX: 6

ERUPTION TYPE: Plinian/Ultra-Plinian

ERUPTIVE VOLUME: 5 cubic miles (20 km³)

DEATH TOLL: 36,417

Ocean blast

An intense cloud of gas and ash shoots 50 miles (80 km) up from Earth's surface during the final cataclysmic eruption at Krakatau. There were four huge explosions that occurred over a period of about four hours. The final explosion was the biggest of all.

Krakatau

Krakatau finally blew its top in August 1883 after three months of intensifying activity. The eruption made the loudest sound probably ever heard by humans and rates as the most powerful volcanic explosion ever witnessed. The eruption obliterated the volcanic cone of Krakatau and destroyed the island on which it sat. Many thousands of people were killed when tsunamis generated by hot pyroclastic flows entering the ocean enveloped the neighboring parts of Indonesia. Ash from the eruption spread around the globe, causing unusually cool weather and glorious sunsets for many months. Today a new volcanic cone, Anak Krakatau, has risen from the seafloor where Krakatau once stood.

Krakatau scream

Volcanic particles high in the atmosphere produced vivid sunsets for months after the eruption. This famous painting by Norwegian Edvard Munch is thought to depict such a sunset seen in Oslo at the opposite side of Earth.

AFTER THE BLAST

Volcanologists are not sure why the Krakatau blast was so big, though it probably was due to an explosive reaction between magma and seawater.

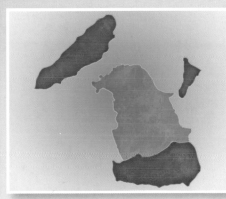

Before and after
In the final stages of the eruption, most of Krakatau Island sank into the sea. The original area of the island is shown as pale green in the map above. Ash deposited in the eruption increased the size of the other islands that ringed the older Krakatau caldera.

Ash and noise pattern
The volcanic ash (gray) from the eruption spread mostly to the northwest. The sounds of the successive volcanic blasts (red) reverberated throughout the region and were heard up to 2,800 miles (4,500 km) away.

VEI 9

VEI 8

VEI 7

VEI 6

VEI 5

VEI 4

VEI 3

VEI 2

VEI 1

MOUNT ST. HELENS: THE FACTS

DATE:	May 18, 1980
VOLCANIC EXPLOSIVITY INDEX:	5
ERUPTION TYPE:	Plinian
ERUPTIVE VOLUME:	0.25 cubic miles (1 km³)
DEATH TOLL:	57

Mount St. Helens today
This photo shows the huge crater blasted out of the mountain summit in the eruption. At the center of the crater, a periodically active lava dome has slowly grown over the magma channel to the surface.

Mount St. Helens

The United States' worst volcanic disaster is also one of the world's best recorded and most comprehensively studied eruptions. When Mount St. Helens violently erupted in 1980 after lying dormant for 120 years, no one was really surprised. Scientists had been closely watching the volcano for months, and although they could not predict the exact date of the eruption, they knew the growing bulge on the mountain's side could only mean that magma was moving upward and that an eruption was imminent. The blast ripped a huge hole in the top and side of the once cone-shaped volcano, flattened forests for miles around, and rained ash over a large swath of the northwestern United States and as far away as Oklahoma.

1 **March–May 1980** *Over several months magma welled up into the volcano, producing a conspicuous bulge of fractured rock on its north flank. Scientists had been watching the ground deform and recording earthquakes for weeks before the eruption.*

2 **08:32:37, May 18** *Finally, the volcano flank gave way, producing a huge landslide and volcanic blasts at both the summit and side of the mountain. Geologists have used features of this well-observed landslide to identify similar deposits at many other volcanoes.*

Blowing its top

Video footage revealed that once the eruption began, it took less than a minute for the bulk of Mount St. Helens to be blasted away in a cataclysmic explosion.

3 **08:32:41, May 18** *The crater blasted wide open and a huge column of rock, ash, and gas was thrown up and out of Mount St. Helens' summit, feeding pyroclastic flows and a mushroom cloud that reached 12 miles (19 km) into the atmosphere.*

Urban ash fall

Fallout of volcanic ash spread east in the days after the eruption and affected many towns in the Pacific Northwest. Fortunately, the nearby cities of Portland and Seattle were mostly spared.

A forest flattened

Trees were scattered like toothpicks as hundreds of square miles of forest were flattened by the volcanic blast racing down the mountain's slopes.

Lahar flow

Within 15 minutes of the eruption, a hot flow of volcanic ash and water, called a lahar, rushed down from the mountain. It was recorded traveling at 44 miles per hour (71 km/h).

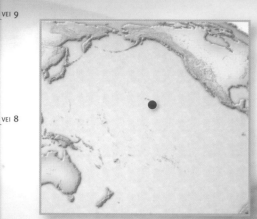

KILAUEA: THE FACTS

DATE: 1983–present

VOLCANIC EXPLOSIVITY INDEX: 1

ERUPTION TYPE: **Hawaiian**

ERUPTIVE VOLUME: 0.7 cubic miles (3 km³)

DEATH TOLL: Several careless visitors have died from exposure to gases or from falls

Kilauea crater

Halema'uma'u pit crater, 280 feet deep by 3,000 feet wide (85 m x 915 m), has been the source of many of Kilauea's historical eruptions. It lies within the much larger, nearly circular, Kilauea summit caldera.

Kilauea Caldera

Kilauea

Nestled in the southeastern corner of the Big Island of Hawaii, in the middle of the Pacific Ocean, is Kilauea, one of the world's most active volcanoes. It has erupted nearly 50 times in the past century and has been erupting nearly continuously since 1983. Most eruptions at Kilauea are relatively gentle, producing spectacular fire fountains and long lava flows. This quiet eruptive behavior has earned Kilauea the nickname of "the drive-up volcano" because thousands of visitors come face-to-face with flowing lava there each year. But make no mistake; even "calm" volcanoes like Kilauea are potentially dangerous and destructive.

Kilauea from space

From space Kilauea is revealed nestled against the tallest active volcano on Earth, Mauna Loa. The reddish-brown areas are where young lava flows have covered the otherwise lush tropical landscape.

Summit magma reservoir

Eruptions are fed by a pool of rising magma that collects about 2 miles (3 km) below the surface.

Eruption

In the early days of the Pu'u O'o eruption, fire fountains of molten lava spurted up to 1,600 feet (500 m) into the air from a 4.5-mile- (7-km) long fissure.

Destruction

The advancing lava flows have buried large areas of national parkland, destroyed 189 homes, and forced the rerouting of several roads.

Lava meets ocean

Surface and tube-fed lava flows have traveled the nearly 6 miles (10 km) from the Pu'u O'o and Kupaianaha vents to enter the sea in a fiery display almost continuously since late 1986.

Napau crater 1983, 1997

Pu'u O'o

Lava tube

Kupaianaha vents, 1986

Lava tube outlet

Kilauea dissected

This cutaway view shows the Kilauea magma chamber and subterranean magma delivery system to the East Rift Zone, where the Pu'u O'o eruption has been occurring for the past 25 years. Magma gushes upward, erupts at the surface, and flows downslope to the sea.

LISBON: THE FACTS

DATE: November 1, 1755

DURATION: 3.5–6 minutes

RICHTER SCALE: Estimated 8–9

MERCALLI SCALE: X (disastrous)

DEATH TOLL: 60,000–100,000

Lisbon

Earth's crust ruptured 120 miles (190 km) offshore from Lisbon, Portugal, on November 1, 1755, unleashing one of history's deadliest seismic disasters. Great buildings collapsed, large fissures opened up in city streets, a tsunami and then a fire raced through the city. Portugal's colonial ambitions were crippled. But with this terrible destruction came the beginnings of modern earthquake science. Rather than simply attributing the destruction to an act of God, Portugal's government instructed priests throughout the country to survey the damage and report on the population's experiences so that the nature of the earthquake could be better understood.

REBUILDING LISBON

Braced within
Timber bracing embedded within masonry walls helped prevent walls from collapsing.

Lisbon had to be almost completely rebuilt after the 1755 earthquake. For the first time in modern Europe, strict building rules were enforced to ensure that the new city could better withstand earthquake forces.

Cage frames
At the heart of the new buildings of downtown Lisbon were intricate timber frames that could safely dissipate seismic energy.

Wave of destruction
About half an hour after the quake, a massive tsunami crashed into Lisbon's harbor. Unfortunately, this is where many survivors had gathered, fearful that aftershocks would bring down more buildings in the city.

THE SAN FRANCISCO EARTHQUAKE

DATE: April 18, 1906

DURATION: 45–60 seconds

RICHTER SCALE: 7.8–8.3

MERCALLI SCALE: VII–IX

DEATH TOLL: 478 (official); 3,000–6,000 (estimated)

Disaster at dawn

San Franciscans awoke just after 5:00 a.m. April 18, 1906, to a violent shaking that was felt as far away as Los Angeles. Within a minute, the city was destroyed. Geologists had never seen such extensive ground rupturing or observed such differences in the severity of ground shaking, which was worst in areas with sediments and soils and much less severe in areas on bedrock. This gave them new understanding of earthquake hazards and how to use this knowledge for urban planning.

San Francisco

The city of San Francisco, California, sits astride the great San Andreas Fault, where the Pacific Plate grinds up against the North American Plate. The San Francisco region owes its rugged beauty to the geological forces of this continental margin. Deep below the city great frictional stresses build up within Earth's crust. Small earthquakes happen many times a year to relieve some of the stress, but occasionally a great earthquake occurs, as it did one morning in 1906, when perhaps as many as 6,000 people lost their lives.

Road chasm *All across the city giant cracks opened in the earth, resulting in broken gas lines and burst water pipes.*

SAN FRANCISCO ABLAZE

Most of the destruction of the 1906 earthquake resulted not from the earthquake itself but the subsequent fires that swept through the city, which burned for four days and four nights.

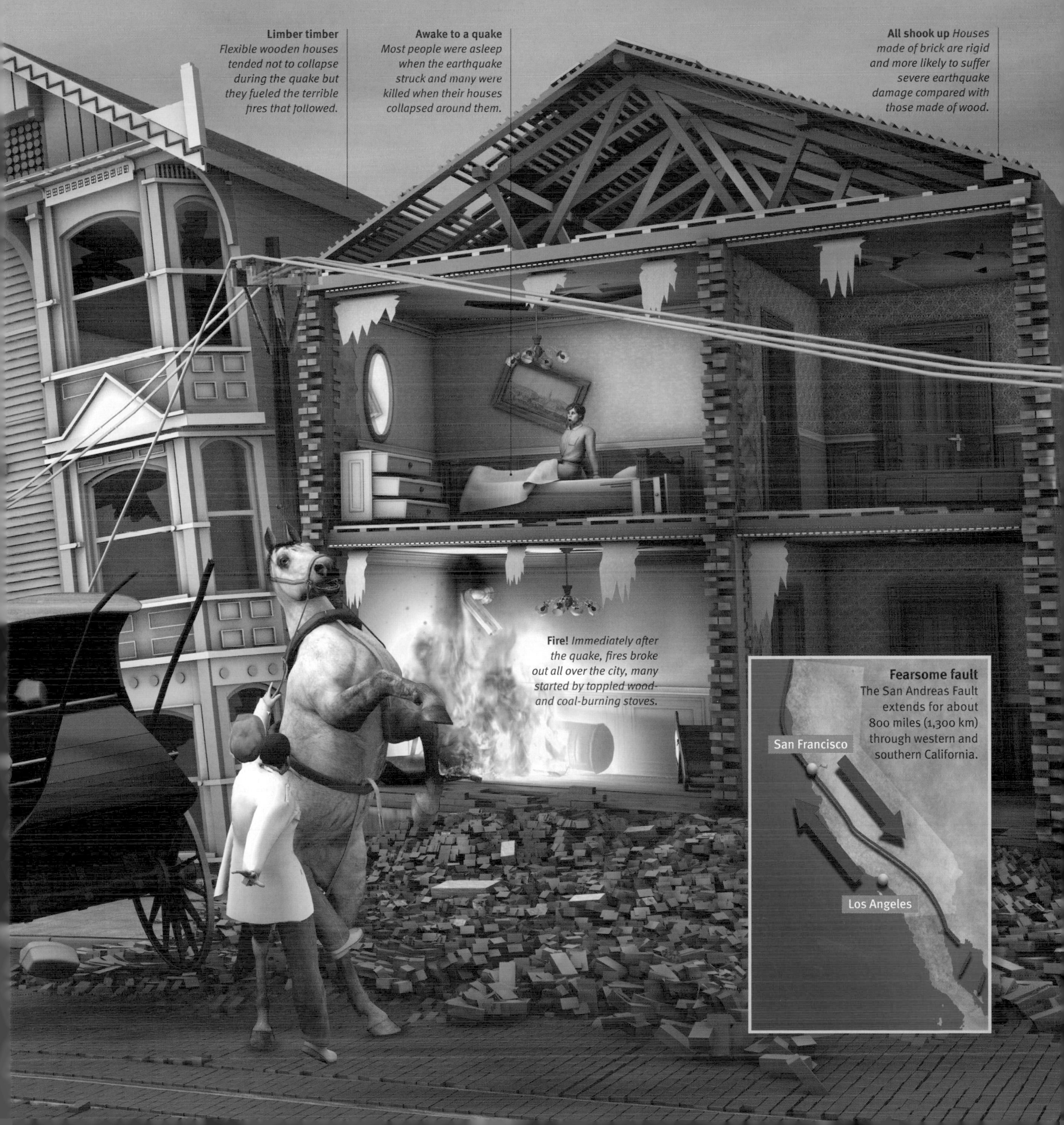

Limber timber
Flexible wooden houses tended not to collapse during the quake but they fueled the terrible fires that followed.

Awake to a quake
Most people were asleep when the earthquake struck and many were killed when their houses collapsed around them.

All shook up *Houses made of brick are rigid and more likely to suffer severe earthquake damage compared with those made of wood.*

Fire! *Immediately after the quake, fires broke out all over the city, many started by toppled wood- and coal-burning stoves.*

Fearsome fault
The San Andreas Fault extends for about 800 miles (1,300 km) through western and southern California.

San Francisco

Los Angeles

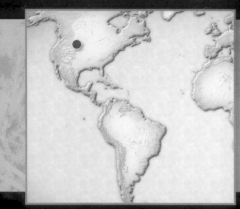

HEBGEN LAKE, MONTANA: THE FACTS

DATE: August 17, 1959

DURATION: 30–45 seconds

RICHTER SCALE: 7.5

MERCALLI SCALE: X (disastrous)

DEATH TOLL: 28

Stages of disaster

In just a few moments the landscape of the Madison River Canyon area was radically and permanently altered.

1 As the earthquake struck, the land north of Hebgen Lake moved upward in a sudden jolt, creating a fault scarp 20 feet (6 m) high.

Hebgen Lake

Earthquakes have the power to permanently alter the landscape. One striking example is the Hebgen Lake earthquake that struck a remote corner of rural Montana, United States, in 1959. The ground ruptured more than 20 feet (6 m) in places, and the quake produced a huge landslide that raced down the side of Madison Canyon, damming the Madison River and burying 28 campers. The waters of nearby Lake Hebgen were shaken like a rocking bathtub, and a wave crested its concrete dam four times. New hot springs and geysers sprung up in nearby Yellowstone National Park. Over the following month, accumulating water formed a new lake, called Earthquake Lake, behind the new earthen dam.

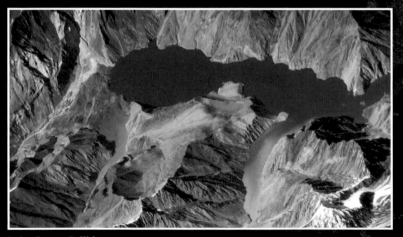

Lake Sarez, Tajikistan

In 1911 a powerful earthquake and landslide in Tajikistan, central Asia, created the largest dam in the world, man-made or natural. The resulting lake is 38 miles (61 km) long and up to 1,600 feet (500 m) deep. There are fears that another earthquake could break the dam and put millions of lives downstream in danger.

Mountain in motion

Because the earthquake struck in a remote area, the death toll was relatively low for such a powerful quake. However, 28 unfortunate vacationers lost their lives when the landslide overran the Rock Creek Campground.

2 A massive face of a mountain at the side of Madison Canyon broke free, sending an avalanche of rocks down to the river below. Meanwhile, waves generated by suddenly tilted ground beneath Hebgen Lake surged over the lake's concrete dam.

3 Landslide debris came to rest on the canyon floor, damming the Madison River and forming a new lake. Engineers later removed some of this material and formed a spillway to lower the lake and reduce the risk of the dam breaking.

KOBE, JAPAN: THE FACTS

DATE: January 17, 1995

DURATION: 20 seconds

RICHTER SCALE: 6.9–7.3

MERCALLI SCALE: X–XII (disastrous–catastrophic)

DEATH TOLL: 6,434

Seismic map of Japan

The Kobe earthquake occurred when a strike-slip fault ruptured just north and west of the main seismic zone that skirts Japan's eastern coastline. Although virtually all of Japan is earthquake-prone, Kobe lies in a less active area and was considered relatively safe from major earthquakes. This map shows selected earthquakes recorded in Japan from 1961 to 1994. The bigger the circle, the more powerful the earthquake. Shallow earthquakes tend to be more powerful and destructive than ones which originate from deep within Earth.

EURASIAN PLATE

Kobe

Tokyo

PACIFIC PLATE

PHILLIPPINE PLATE

Depth of hypocenter
- 0–31 miles (0–50 km)
- 31–62 miles (50–100 km)
- 62–93 miles (100–150 km)
- 93–124 miles (150–200 km)

Kobe

Early one morning in January 1995, residents of Kobe, Japan, were startled awake when a fierce earthquake nearly leveled their city. The quake struck near Awaji Island, where the ground heaved up 9 feet (3 m) during surface rupture of the fault. The seismic waves raced through the crust to Kobe, 12 miles (20 km) away, causing one of the most costly natural disasters ever. The damage was extensive because the epicenter was so close to a large and densely populated city. Even worse, Kobe had been considered at low risk for severe earthquakes, and building codes were not as strict as in other parts of Japan.

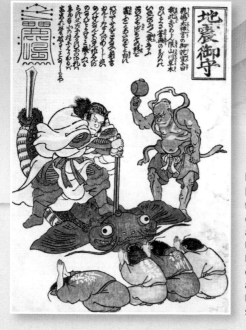

Namazu and Kashima Traditionally, the Japanese blamed earthquakes on Namazu, a subterranean catfish. Usually the deity Kashima held Namazu down, but if Kashima's attention wandered, Namazu thrashed about, shaking the ground.

1 Intact column In the reinforced columns, steel and concrete work together. Concrete supports the huge weight of the expressway while steel rods hold the concrete together and keep the forces vertical all along the length of the column.

2 Earthquake The columns are not nearly so strong when horizontal forces are applied. During the earthquake small cracks begin to open and the bond between the steel and concrete is weakened.

Expressway collapse

The elevated Hanshin Expressway was hard hit by the earthquake, with damage to half of its concrete piers. Ten separate spans collapsed completely.

City in ruins

Factories, offices, schools, and countless homes were all damaged beyond repair. More than six thousand Kobe residents were killed and another three hundred thousand people, one-third of the city's population, were left homeless.

3 Failure point As more concrete crumbles, only the steel rods support the expressway. They quickly buckle and twist, and the whole structure collapses.

INDIAN OCEAN TSUNAMI: THE FACTS

DATE: December 26, 2004

DURATION: 10 minutes

RICHTER SCALE: 9.3

MERCALLI SCALE: XI (very disastrous)

DEATH TOLL: Approximately 230,000

Earth shaker

This was a disaster of global proportions. Lives were lost on the shores of 13 nations, and citizens from a total of 55 nations were killed. The disaster took hours to unfold. The lines and numbers on the globe indicate how far the tsunami traveled each hour after the earthquake.

Kerala, India *Tsunami waves can diffract around a landmass and change direction. Hundreds of people died on the "sheltered" west coast of India.*

Indian Ocean

Tsunami

The whole Earth vibrated like a bell when the second largest earthquake ever recorded struck on December 26, 2004. The enormous, undersea Sumatra–Andaman earthquake lasted 10 minutes—the longest on record—and ruptured nearly 1,000 miles (1,600 km) of seabed. The quake unleashed a series of tsunamis that devastated coastlines all around the Indian Ocean and killed hundreds of thousands of people in Southeast Asia. Sadly, many would have survived had a multinational tsunami early-warning system been in place. Such a system is only now being established in the Indian Ocean.

Sea to sky The data is relayed to satellite.

Sky to ground The satellite transmits data to ground stations.

Tsunami early warning systems

With the right technology in place, advanced warning of a tsunami's approach can be relayed from the open ocean back to shore. Communities at risk can then be alerted via sirens, radio and television broadcasts, and cell phone messages.

Seafloor up The data is transmitted to a buoy on the surface.

Tsunameter At the heart of the system is a pressure sensor on the seabed. It can detect tsunami waves as small as 0.4 inches (1 cm).

c. 20,000 feet (6,000 m)

Port Elizabeth, South Africa *The most distant death attributed to the tsunami was a drowning in Port Elizabeth, about 5,000 miles (8,000 km) from the epicenter.*

Andaman and Nicobar Islands *This island group was shifted southwest by about 4 feet (1.25 m).*

Thailand *More than 2,000 foreign tourists died on vacation in Thailand. But everyone survived on one beach, thanks to a 10-year-old girl who recognized the warning signs and told people to seek higher ground.*

Epicenter *The earthquake epicenter was located where the Indian Plate subducts under the Burma Plate.*

Simeulue *Few people died on the closest island to the epicenter. From memories of a 1907 tsunami, locals knew to move inland when they felt the earthquake. The island was pushed up by 4.9 feet (1.5 m).*

Pacific *Some energy escaped to the Pacific, where it produced small tsunami waves along the North and South American coasts.*

In a spin *Scientists estimate that Earth wobbled on its axis by about 1 inch (2.5 cm).*

Banda Aceh after the waves

Banda Aceh, on the western tip of Sumatra in Indonesia, was the closest city to the earthquake epicenter. The tsunami waves washed away almost all of the buildings in the city. Tens of thousands died.

Stranded boats

The local fishing fleet was strewn across the landscape by the waves. These boats came to rest about two miles (3 km) inland.

Seabed uplift

The tsunami waves were powered by a rupture in the seabed hundreds of miles long. On average, one side of the rupture came to rest 16 feet (5 m) higher than the other. In some places the difference was as much as 65 feet (20 m).

1

Worlds Alive

VOLCANOES AROUND THE WORLD

Volcano map

There are about 1,500 active volcanoes around the world and many more that are dormant or extinct. This map shows some notable examples.

Legend

▲ = Active volcano

△ = Dormant volcano

▲ = Extinct volcano

▲ = Height

✳ = Last eruption

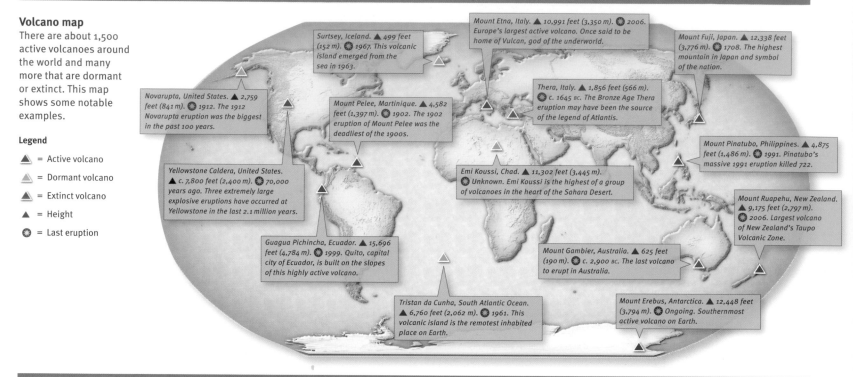

Surtsey, Iceland. ▲ 499 feet (152 m). ✳ 1967. This volcanic island emerged from the sea in 1963.

Mount Etna, Italy. ▲ 10,991 feet (3,350 m). ✳ 2006. Europe's largest active volcano. Once said to be home of Vulcan, god of the underworld.

Mount Fuji, Japan. ▲ 12,338 feet (3,776 m). ✳ 1708. The highest mountain in Japan and symbol of the nation.

Novarupta, United States. ▲ 2,759 feet (841 m). ✳ 1912. The 1912 Novarupta eruption was the biggest in the past 100 years.

Mount Pelee, Martinique. ▲ 4,582 feet (1,397 m). ✳ 1902. The 1902 eruption of Mount Pelee was the deadliest of the 1900s.

Thera, Italy. ▲ 1,856 feet (566 m). ✳ c. 1645 BC. The Bronze Age Thera eruption may have been the source of the legend of Atlantis.

Mount Pinatubo, Philippines. ▲ 4,875 feet (1,486 m). ✳ 1991. Pinatubo's massive 1991 eruption killed 722.

Yellowstone Caldera, United States. ▲ c. 7,800 feet (2,400 m). ✳ 70,000 years ago. Three extremely large explosive eruptions have occurred at Yellowstone in the last 2.1 million years.

Emi Koussi, Chad. ▲ 11,302 feet (3,445 m). ✳ Unknown. Emi Koussi is the highest of a group of volcanoes in the heart of the Sahara Desert.

Mount Ruapehu, New Zealand. ▲ 9,175 feet (2,797 m). ✳ 2006. Largest volcano of New Zealand's Taupo Volcanic Zone.

Guagua Pichincha, Ecuador. ▲ 15,696 feet (4,784 m). ✳ 1999. Quito, capital city of Ecuador, is built on the slopes of this highly active volcano.

Mount Gambier, Australia. ▲ 625 feet (190 m). ✳ c. 2,900 BC. The last volcano to erupt in Australia.

Tristan da Cunha, South Atlantic Ocean. ▲ 6,760 feet (2,062 m). ✳ 1961. This volcanic island is the remotest inhabited place on Earth.

Mount Erebus, Antarctica. ▲ 12,448 feet (3,794 m). ✳ Ongoing. Southernmost active volcano on Earth.

EARTHQUAKE RISK

Earthquake map

The chances of being shaken up by an earthquake depend on where on Earth you are. In many places you could live a whole lifetime and never feel the ground move. In other places, tremors are a regular occurrence and the risk of a destructive earthquake is always present.

Earthquake risk

= Low

= Medium

= High

= Very high

EARTHQUAKE THEORIES

Changing ideas

As long as people have felt the ground shake, they have sought to explain the frightening phenomenon of earthquakes. But it is only very recently that we have truly worked out what is happening beneath our feet.

A Hindu cosmos.

Religious and mythical explanations

For centuries, explanations for earthquakes were linked with religion and myth. For instance, according to an ancient Hindu myth, Earth is carried on the back of an elephant, which stands on a turtle that is balanced on a cobra. Whenever one moves, Earth trembles and shakes.

Ancient Greeks

The ancient Greek philosophers are the first people we know of to seek natural explanations for earthquakes. They speculated that within Earth there are vast caverns where wild winds blow. Earth shakes when the winds blow on the cavern roofs or break through to the surface.

A cross section of Earth's interior from 1665.

Early modern Europe

The Italian artist and inventor Leonardo da Vinci theorized that Earth was composed of solid matter interspersed with water. If the balance between them is upset, sudden movements occur. In the 1660s the French philosopher René Descartes suggested that Earth was once as hot as the Sun and that it is still cooling and shrinking. These contractions created the mountains and cause earthquakes.

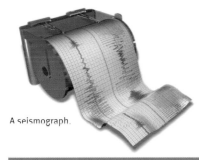

A seismograph.

Modern times

Plate tectonic theory had its beginnings in 1915, when German scientist Alfred Wegener suggested that all the continents were once joined together and had subsequently drifted apart. This would explain why the outlines of the continents so often seem to fit together like a puzzle. Wegener could not explain how the continents moved, but research in the 1950s and 60s revealed the existence of tectonic plates and seafloor spreading. Plate tectonic theory has proved to be a convincing explanation for earthquakes and other geological phenomena.

VOLCANOES OUT OF THIS WORLD

Space shaper

Volcanoes are not restricted to Earth. In fact, judging by our own Solar System, volcanism seems to be quite a common phenomenon in the universe. Volcanoes have played a part in shaping the surface of all four inner rocky planets (Mercury, Venus, Earth, and Mars) as well as some of the moons of the outer gas giants.

The Moon
Billions of years ago Earth's moon was volcanically active. The dark patches we can see on the surface are solidified lakes of molten lava.

Venus
Venus has many thousands of volcanoes. They are responsible for the planet's thick atmosphere. Scientists are not sure if any volcanoes are still active.

Mars
Mars is about half the size of Earth, but it boasts volcanoes that dwarf the tallest mountains on our planet. However, Mars is almost certainly volcanically extinct.

Io
Jupiter's moon Io is the most volcanically active body in the Solar System. It spews a noxious mixture of molten and gaseous sulfur dioxide from its surface.

Triton
Volcanoes are not always hot. In 1989 a passing space probe discovered huge geysers on Neptune's moon Triton that erupt with supercold liquid nitrogen.

INDIAN OCEAN TSUNAMI

Dead or missing by nationality

	1–10	11–100	101–1,000	1,001–10,000	10,001–100,000	100,001–200,000
* Indonesia: 167,540						
* Sri Lanka: 35,322						
* India: 16,269						
* Thailand: 5,996						
Germany: 552						
Sweden: 543						
* Somalia: 289						
Finland: 178						
United Kingdom: 149						
Switzerland: 111						
* Maldives: 108						
France: 95						
Norway: 84						
* Malaysia: 75						
Austria: 74						
* Myanmar: 61						
Japan: 44						
Italy: 40						
Hong Kong: 40						
Netherlands: 36						
United States: 31						
Australia: 26						
* South Africa: 23						
South Korea: 20						
Canada: 20						
* Tanzania: 13						
Belgium: 11						
China: 10						
* Seychelles: 2						
* Bangladesh: 2						
* Kenya: 1						

* = countries directly affected by the tsunami. (Note that 21 of the South African dead were killed in Thailand.)

Geysers around Neptune

This illustration shows Triton's geysers erupting with plumes of liquid nitrogen. This material rises about five miles (8 km) above the surface before raining down as nitrogen frost.

Glossary

a'a A type of lava flow that has a jagged surface when it cools and solidifies.

active volcano A volcano that produces eruptions of gas and lava. The bursts may be separated by weeks or many centuries.

aerosol Small particles and liquid droplets formed as volcanic gases cool in the air.

aftershock A tremor that follows a large earthquake and originates at or near the hypocenter of the initial quake.

ash Fine pieces of rock and lava ejected during volcanic eruptions.

asthenosphere A layer in Earth's upper mantle so soft that it can flow.

black smoker A vent situated on an ocean ridge, which emits hot, mineral-laden water.

caldera A large, circular depression formed when a volcano collapses above its magma chamber.

cinder Small fragments of volcanic rock, usually full of trapped gas bubbles, ejected during a volcanic eruption. Also called scoria.

conduit A wide pipe inside a volcano through which magma moves from the interior to a vent.

continent One of Earth's seven main landmasses: Africa, Antarctica, Asia, Australia, Europe, North America, and South America. The landmasses include edges beneath the ocean as well as dry land.

continental margin The edges of continental landmasses consisting of the coastal zone and shallowly submerged lands near the coast.

convection current A current that transfers heat by moving material around, such as the movement of hot rock in the mantle.

convergent margin A boundary between two tectonic plates that are moving toward each other.

core Earth's center. It consists of a solid inner core and a molten outer core, both of which are made of an iron-nickel alloy.

crater A circular depression formed as a result of a volcanic eruption (volcanic crater) or by the impact of a meteorite (impact crater).

crater lake A water-filled crater. It may be filled on a seasonal or permanent basis.

crust The outermost solid layer of Earth, which varies from a thickness of 3 miles (5 km), under the youngest seafloor, to 45 miles (72 km), under the thickest parts of continents.

dike A sheet of igneous rock formed when magma rises through a crack.

divergent margin A boundary between two tectonic plates that are moving apart.

dormant volcano A volcano that is not currently active but that could erupt again.

epicenter The point on Earth's surface that is directly above the hypocenter, or starting point, of an earthquake.

eruption The volcanic release of lava, ash, or gas from Earth's interior onto the surface and into the atmosphere.

extinct volcano A volcano that has shown no sign of activity for a long period and is considered unlikely to erupt again.

fault margin A crack in rock layers created by the rocks shifting in opposite directions or at different speeds.

fissure A fracture or crack in the ground. In volcanic areas, a fissure may be associated with a line of vents (known as fissure volcanoes).

flood basalt A flow of basalt lava that spreads over a large area. Many layers of these flows form a basalt plateau.

fumarole A vent that emits hot volcanic gases or steam.

geologist A scientist who studies the physical and chemical processes that have shaped Earth's surface and interior today or in the past.

geothermal energy Energy that can be extracted from Earth's interior heat, whether from hot rocks, hot water, or steam.

geyser A surface vent that periodically spouts a fountain of boiling water.

hot spot A persistent and nearly stationary zone of melting within Earth's mantle.

hydrothermal activity Any process involving the formation or movement of water and dissolved chemicals by interaction with hot rock.

hypocenter The place within Earth where energy in strained rocks is suddenly released as earthquake waves.

igneous Rock formed when magma cools and solidifies.

island arc An arc-shaped chain of volcanic islands that forms above subducting seafloor.

laccolith A body of igneous rock formed when rising magma cools before erupting at the surface. Laccoliths often push overlying rock layers upward.

lahar A flow of hot mud created by a volcanic eruption.

lateral fault A fault along which rocks have moved sideways. It is sometimes called a strike-slip or transform fault.

lava Molten rock that has erupted from a volcano onto Earth's surface.

lava bomb A large lump of molten lava or hot rock thrown from a volcano that attains a nearly spherical shape as it cools in flight. A lava bomb is usually more than 1.25 inches (32 mm) across.

lava dome A mound of thick, sticky lava that grows directly over a vent at the top of, or on the flanks of, a volcano.

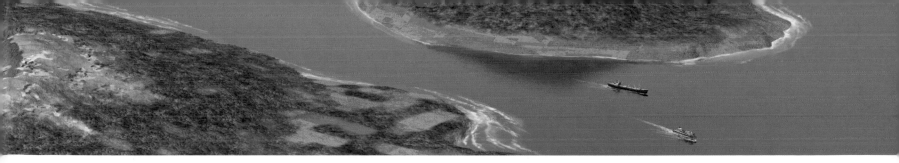

lava tube An underground river of lava formed when the surface of an open lava channel solidifies.

liquefaction The change of sediment or soil into a fluid mass as a result of an earthquake.

lithosphere The rigid outer part of Earth, consisting of the crust and the uppermost part of the mantle.

magma Melted rock found inside Earth. It may solidify inside Earth or erupt at the surface to form lava.

magma chamber A pool of magma in the lithosphere from which volcanic materials may erupt.

magnitude The strength of an earthquake, based on the amount of energy released. Seismologists measure magnitude using the modified Richter Scale, which begins at zero and has no maximum.

mantle The thick layer between Earth's crust and the outer core. It includes the lower mantle and asthenosphere—the parts of the mantle that flow—and the lower lithosphere, which is the rigid uppermost part of the mantle.

mid-ocean ridge A long, raised ridge formed by volcanic action at the edges of diverging oceanic plates.

mineral A naturally formed solid with an ordered arrangement of atoms, found in Earth's crust.

mudflow A river of ash, mud, and water set off by a volcanic eruption or earthquake. Mudflows triggered by volcanoes are also known as lahars.

normal fault A fracture in rock layers, where the upper side has moved downward relative to the other side along a plane inclined between 45 and 90 degrees.

pahoehoe A type of lava flow with a smooth, ropelike surface.

pillow lava Lava that forms rounded mounds by cooling quickly after erupting underwater or flowing into water.

plug A column of volcanic rock formed when lava solidifies inside the vent of a volcano.

plume A rising column of hot rock in the mantle, within which melting can take place. The term can also apply to a large column of ash above a volcano.

primary wave A seismic wave, also known as a P-wave, that compresses and expands rocks as it travels through them. It is called a primary wave because it is the wave that arrives first during an earthquake, before the secondary wave.

pumice A light-colored, low-density, glassy volcanic rock that contains many cavities. It is so light that it can float in water.

pyroclastic flow A dense, heated mixture of volcanic gas, ash, and rock fragments that travels at great speed down volcanic slopes. It forms as a result of the collapse of an eruption column or a lava dome.

reverse fault A fracture in rock layers, where the top side has moved upward relative to the other side along a plane inclined between 45 and 90 degrees.

rift valley A wide valley that forms when rock layers move apart and a central section drops downward as a result of normal faulting.

secondary wave A seismic wave, also known as an S-wave, that moves rocks from side to side as it passes through them. It is called a secondary wave because it is the second type of wave to arrive during an earthquake.

seismic Related to an earthquake or tremor.

seismologist A scientist who studies seismic waves produced by earthquakes to understand where and how they form or to study Earth's internal and surface structure.

seismology The study of Earth tremors, whether natural or artificially produced.

seismometer An instrument that detects, magnifies, and records Earth's vibrations.

shield volcano A volcano that is much wider than it is tall, formed by repeated flows of lava. This type of volcano looks like a shield when viewed from above.

subduction The process in which one tectonic plate descends below another.

subterranean Related to things that are found or that occur underground.

surface wave A seismic wave that travels along Earth's surface. It arrives after primary and secondary waves and moves up and down or from side to side.

tectonic plate Rigid pieces of Earth's lithosphere that move over the asthenosphere.

tephra Particles or fragments ejected from a volcano of any size or shape.

thrust fault A fracture in rock layers, where the upper side rides over the top of the lower side at an angle of less than 45 degrees.

transform fault A fault along which rocks move in opposite directions or at different speeds. They are common at some plate margins.

tsunami A Japanese word for a sea wave produced by an earthquake, landslide, or volcanic blast. It reaches its greatest height in shallow waters before crashing onto land.

vent An opening on the surface of a volcano through which lava and gas erupt.

volcano A typically circular landform from which molten rock and gases erupt.

volcanologist A scientist who studies eruptions and interior processes at active and inactive volcanoes.

Index

Credits

The publisher thanks Alexandra Cooper for her contribution,
and Puddingburn for the index.

ILLUSTRATIONS
Front cover Peter Bull Art Studio (Main), GODD.com (support);
back cover GODD.com tr, Peter Bull Art Studio bl, Mark A. Garlick b
GODD.com 4, 30–1, 38–9, 52–3, 56–7; **Peter Bull Art Studio** 1, 4, 5, 6–7,
10–11, 18–19, 20–1, 22–3, 24–5, 26–7, 28–9, 32–3, 36–7, 40–1, 42–3,
46–7, 48–9, 50–1, 54–5, 58–9, 60–1; **Mark A. Garlick** 3, 4, 5, 8–9, 12–13,
14–15, 16–17, 44–5, 58–9, 61 bl, bcr; **Moonrunner Design** 34–5;
Steven Hobbs 61 c; **Steve Trevaskis** 61 tl

MAPS
Map Illustrations, Andrew Davies

PHOTOGRAPHS
Key l=left, r=right, tl=top left, tcl=top center left, tc=top center, tcr=top
center right, tr=top right, cl=center left, c=center, cr=center right, b=bottom,
bl=bottom left, bcl=bottom center left, bc=bottom center, bcr=bottom
center right, br=bottom right

AA=The Art Archive; AAP=Australian Associated Press; APL=Australian
Picture Library; CBT=Corbis; iS=iStock; MEPL=Mary Evans Picture Library;
N_J=NASA/Jet Propulsion Laboratory; N_L=NASA Landsat; N_V=NASA/Visible
Earth; PL=photolibrary.com

10cl N_V; **14**tr N_V; **21**br AAP; **24**bl APL; **27**tc, tl PL; **33**br CBT; **40**bl N_L; **44**bl
AA; **46**tr CBT; **48**bl, tr CBT; **49**tl, tcl, tcr, tr CBT; **54**bl N_V; **56**bl Gregory Smits;
57tr CBT; **59**cr, tr CBT; **61**bcl, bl, c N_J; cl iS; tc MEPL